for my son Zaphyr
and in memory of my mother Julia

Half of what I say is meaningless; but I say it
so that the other half may reach you
    – KHALIL GIBRAN, *Sand and Foam*

Contents

US

If on a sunny day you climb the steep path leading up from the little wooden bridge still referred to around here as 'the Bridge of Hesitation', you will not have to walk far before the roof of my house becomes visible . . .

– KAZUO ISHIGURO, *An Artist of the Floating World*

.

Fielder

If I had to put my finger on where this started,
I'd trace a circle round the one moment I came to, or the one
that placed me, a fielder, just past the field, over the rope,
having chased a lost cause, leathered for six . . .
when, bumbling about, obscured in the bushes,
I completely stopped looking for the ball –
perhaps irresponsibly – slowed by bracken, caught by light
that slipped the dark cordon of rhododendron hands,
a world hidden from the batsmen, the umpires and my team,
like the thing itself: that small, seamed planet, shined
on one half, having reached its stop, out of the sphere of sight.
And when I reflect, here, from this undiscovered city,
well north of those boyish ambitions – for the county,
maybe later, the country – I know something of that minute
holds something of me, there, beyond the boundary,
in that edgeland of central England. A shady fingernail
of forest. The pitch it points at, or past, a stopped clock.
Still, in the middle, the keeper's gloves
clap at the evening. Still, a train clicks
on far-off tracks. And the stars are still to surface.
The whole field, meanwhile, waiting for me,
some astronaut, or lost explorer, to emerge with a wave
that brings the ball   like time itself   to hand. A world restored.
But what I'd come to find, in that late hour
was out of mind, and, the thing is, I didn't care
and this is what's throwing me now.

The Word

I couldn't tell you now what possessed me
to shut summer out and stay in my room.
Or at least attempt to. In bed mostly.
It's my dad, standing in the door frame
not entering – but pausing to shape advice
that keeps coming back. 'Whatever is matter,

must *enjoy the life.*' He pronounced this twice.
And me, I heard wrongness in putting a *the*

before *life*. In two minds. Ashamed. Aware.
That I knew better, though was stuck inside
while the sun was out. That I'm native here.
In a halfway house. Like that sticking word.
That definite article, half right, half
wrong, still present between *enjoy* and *life*.

Prayer

First heard words, delivered to this right ear
Allah hu Akbar – God is great – by my father
in the Queen Elizabeth maternity ward.
God's breath in man returning to his birth,
says Herbert, is prayer. If I continued

his lines from there, from *birth* – a break Herbert
chimes with *heav'n and earth* – I'd keep in thought
my mum on a Hereford hospital bed
and say what prayer couldn't end. I'd say
I made an animal noise, hurled language's hurt

at midday, when word had come. Cancer. Now, so spread
by midnight her rings were off.
                              I stayed on. At her bed.
Earlier, time and rhythm flatlining, I whispered
Thank you   I love you   thank you
                              mouth at her ear.
She stared on, ahead. I won't know if she heard.

Hill Speak

There is no dictionary for my father's language.
His dialect, for a start, is difficult to name.
Even this taxi driver, who talks it, lacks the knowledge.
Some say it's Pahari – 'hill speak' –
others, Potwari, or Pahari-Potwari –
too earthy and scriptless to find a home in books.
This mountain speech is a low language. *Ours*. 'No good.
You should learn speak Urdu.' I'm getting the runaround.

Whatever it is, this talk, going back, did once have a script:
Landa, in the reign of the Buddhists.
. . . So was Dad's speech some kind of Dogri?
Is it Kashmiri? Mirpuri? The differences are lost on me.
I'm told it's part way towards Punjabi,
but what that tongue would call *tuwarda*,
Dad would agree was *tusaanda* –
'yours' –

truly, though there are many dictionaries for the tongue I speak,
it's the close-by things I'm lost to say;
things as pulsed and present as the back of this hand,
never mind stumbling towards some higher plane.
And, either way, even at the rare moment I get towards –
or, thank God, even getting to –
my point, I can't put into words
where I've arrived.

The Path

They're there. To the side.
It's hard not to stare
at the centre of the screen
and the stopped kerb.
Struck. But, dear me, look past
what the worst want you to see
and share. And, dear self, even
when the scene strays far from
headlines, when you've gone,
alone, phoneless, stepping over
limb-like roots, and dips, and glooms
into Nutclough Woods on this
treacherous side of the hill – even still,
look to the verges, where some tiny
pixel-flowered herb, perhaps cleavers,
takes hold at a sharp corner
of the descent, like a half-remembered
snatch of a meme, down
past the path, through the scrolling
of a fern's frayed edges
and where, from a few
dark millimetres of earth
a tumble of heads is clutched
as you turn yours – an anonymous
brightness almost too small
to be there, by the wayside,
unmagnified. *Look for
the helpers*. They're there.

Poppy

Who crops up wherever ground is opened, broken . . .
No, this is not enough.

Who crops up where acidic ground is neutralised – in Belgium
blasted bones and rubble added their twist of lime
turning the disturbed earth red . . .
No, this is not enough.

Then where seeds lay buried, dormant – those older than I am,
catching light, can stir from their long sleep in time,
like history, raising a hand, a head . . .
No, this is not enough.

Remember? Who's there in the first script, on a Mesopotamian
tablet: *Hul* and *Gil* – 'joy flower' – a cuneiform
cocktail, our earliest remedy . . .

Who begot war in China, was named by Arabs *Abou-el-noum*,
'father of sleep'; a bloody sign of love's martyrdom –
gul-e-lala – 'flower of red', in Persian and Urdu . . .

Remember? Beloved of Persephone; also found in the tomb –
like a watch, worn on the wrist – of Tutankhamun,
and on coins issued by Herod . . .
No, this is not enough.

You need more? . . . Who crops up, fringing the banks of Lethe
after Troy; who bridges forgetfulness and memory,
life and death, relief and pain . . .

Who was loved by Coleridge who wished *I could wrap up the view
from my House in a pill of opium & send it to you* – to be
seen, swallowed, whole again . . .
No, this is not enough.

Who is the *minded flower* Shakespeare partly saw, in all the drowsy
syrups of the world – a release from grief that calls for more
far-fetched relief, and, as morphine,

sent your sap through my mother's veins, while she could hear me,
while warmth remained in those hands that first held me,
first calmed my small, fevered brain . . .
No, this is not enough.

Whose pupil is a void dilating with light, its first and last entry –
a compound eye, in whichever form – who sees
the black dot of the beginning . . .

Who's there on that date when all the *1*s meet, looped in a wreath
year upon year, or poked through the eye
of a buttonhole. There. I'm done . . .
No, this is not enough.

Then: *Mother – Mother* – last word of that bleeding, wrecked soldier,
as heard by the last Tommy, the last link to living memory –
spoken for now, like the countless millions

of mouthless dead. There in the underworld. The fallen, heavy
head. The deaths we live with. Enough said. Remember?
This is you. Wake up. You're summoned.

No, this is not enough.

Jute

Twelve, staying in my father's village, one Easter
at the house of his mother and first wife,
I remember one day us all, my part of the family, returning
to see two men sat on the woven beds outside
waiting for my father, drinking water from the metal bowls
that covered the clay pots, carried for miles from the well.
Tall men with long legs. They spoke to my father
in a language even stranger than his. One
phrase they kept repeating,

which to my surprise he could follow.
'They are telling me: This is our house.' *But it's not, Dad.*
It's yours, I said. *Tell them.* 'They are on the road.
It's custom'. They'd been on the road since the Russians
a while ago. They stayed. I remember the vowels of their Pashto.
Mostly their long silences. They lodged on those beds outside,
charpoys, the wooden rickety frames we used for sitting
and sleep. The taut rope pressed its uncomfortable crossings
on my back, my sides, but in the stretched air

I slept well, dreamlessly. The tall Afghans helped cut
that wheat I could see when I woke, in the field between
the mountains and the house, squatting till evening, in sandals
the same way my half-brothers did, with a new-moon shaped knife.
In a fortnight they left, without a word, or taking anything.
But I've thought of them, if not often, their circular, sudden hats
on the horizon, their gaunt, pale, tall stubbornness
when I first saw them. Their seated arrival is always
its own unexpected occasion. *This is our house.*

You

The Electric Telegraph has saved us.
– DONALD MCLEOD, Commissioner, British Punjab

——— *1857. Stop. Send help. Stop. Mutiny to come . . .*
Nine decades shy of the bomb
dropping from the sky on Dad's education
which stopped at the age of *maybe seven.*
'Mutiny', or 'Rebellion'? Words and words
only. And neither his. Or theirs. My dad
in his wordless sleep

would kick Mum in hers. Or in the heat
of the moment, ablaze, lit with drink, he'd
say *After you their Tempest planes bombed my school*
or *You are always king of divide and rule*
or *My hands are tied. My tongue can't make good fist
of speech like you. Because of you.* You. The English
second-person plural. Or singular

who arrived in the world in 1947.
A teacher. Five foot tall. I'd hear her.   *Stop*

Sparkhill

Fight. Fight. Fight. Fight. Fight.

They'd begun the chant before we'd started. And started was the word.
He's gonna start on you. After school. Over there. In Sparkhill Park.
By the slope. They talked it up so much, it happened. They gave me
the word and they gave it to him, Jason Walsh. He wants to start on
you. Neither of us had a problem. What made them do it? We'd come
first or second in school races, same height, curly hair, mid-brown
skin. Friends. Let's see them fight. We both went quiet as gravity after
morning break, and all afternoon, and turned up as the other or the
future seemed to need – on the hill, after the last bell. Starting
was hard. The first punch was a shove – like shoves were our
slow way of talking. Shoving arms became thrown arms. Thrown
arms became wrestling arms. And there was love in the grip

on the fat lip of the   slope. No one else there – not
the arguing parents   not the news, not the crowd,
only ashamed attempts   at anger, or worlds turned
upside down. Which was us   with a crowd shouting us
to tumble as we fought   like in the films. We did.
And when we did, the ground   felt harder than any
fist on my mouth, as clouds   whose names I'd yet to learn
intermingled with grass   liquidly, like a head
in a font, like his head   once, only the liquid
was light – the mute grey clouds   or the crowd's word, as we
turned – *fight*. I tasted turf   and saw sky, tongue-tied light
came up from the ground's mouth   the way I had shaped songs
that morning's assembly.   It's false, no energy
in it. But where's it from?   The big bang, or before?

Whatever it is I'm not feeling it

and don't want to go back up and start again, though that's what I'm
hearing we should do. There, at the foot of the hill, I shove him weakly
away, a shove to say I don't mean it, leave it. I grip the bag I dropped
at the start, a bag with a changed gravity, even the heavy logo, its big
letters – H – E – A – D, and head home, head out of the park, down
the very long Stratford Road. I didn't have the fight in me. Or I didn't
think I had. For a very long time. Until this afternoon's grey – past
the green curtain – and that afternoon's grey, rub two flints behind
my eyes. Two flint clouds that ring a bell, dull and bright. And I sit
down, quite some way from St John's primary school, Sparkhill Park,
and that slope where time felt dense. The opposite of light. And I look
past my knuckles, at it – *it*, the black, up-tilted

keyboard, and on that back-   lit slope, these central blocks –
F – G – H . . . And I start   to type: *Fight. Fight. Fight. Fight*

Spider Trees, Pakistan

During the early 1850s, it sometimes seemed as if the British and the Mughals lived not only in different mental worlds, but almost in different time zones.

– WILLIAM DALRYMPLE, *The Last Mughal*

English mists in subcontinental sun;
the withered veil at Miss Havisham's house;
think of that thought in the brain of John Donne
scrawling *In that the world's contracted thus*;
think of holding-spells catching up with time
the way snow floods the sky in slow suspension;
think, though it's a stretch, like shock-haired Einstein
wedding time and space as lacework tension . . .

With floods in Sindh, and their tenants long stranded,
these trees are warped globes, veiled spectres of silk.
It's these photos that have me, stretched, extended –
glued to a webpage since opening a link –
racking my brain for lines to catch how they carry
the gravities of home.   Worlds I can't marry.

W*nd

When I arrived
I didn't know
the word
for what I was.

I kept arriving.
Butting my head
against the shore.
A head with no word.

And one dayless day, I
heard, or it heard
that what I was
was wind. The one

w*nd   I was
the rumour of my own being.
A groundless rumour
in residence.

*

Sure I said. Sure.
Though I wasn't
and have never
been. Shore I said.

Repeating their word
for where I had brought
them. But no shore
was ever a harbour

for me. Never home
entirely. Where are
all four directions
home? Or when?

Sure. I said sure.
Repeating their word
for this coastal state
where I'm never entirely.

*

W, w, w . . .
Between the wires
weather from elsewhere
becomes ours.

Another aloneness
checks in with us, checks us
where stops meet starts.
Entering like my old stutter.

Perhaps the beginning
was the ultimate abbreviation
or silver cord. Aeolus,
a god with all

vowels but one,
knotted the winds in an ox skin.
All swirling directions a word could go.
But not homeward. West, west.

                    *

Wis, wis. In the beginning
w, w, w   It's the *was*
not *the Word* I stutter at, before I
arrive, in *w* and *s*

at the aleph, or alif
that blows me into being.
To the in of the in. The black
of the star, reversed to when all that

was began, before solar w*nd,
interstellar w*nd,
a first breath from beyond
my bond, my vowel.

A wavering oneness
or wand. One's shyest
earliest wound
unwound.

Early Draft

after Rumi

Was it a lost language, like a breath through grass, darkly,
endlessly seeking after its source? It was not. Gnats. Gnats
were storming through the grass, swerving death, jittery
for wisdom. Which they found in the shape of Solomon.
O Solomon, they said, as one, agitated as one. I, we, are
in bits. You care for the wee ones, right? Well here we, I,
am. I'm, we're, so little, we, I, cannot sign anything of note
and life passes in a smudge. The world uses me, us, badly.
I'm, we're, little more than poxy metaphors for nothing. My,
our, being's so small, the sun runs out of gnat veins too soon.
Look in the middle of resignation! *Slap-bang.* Defend us, me!

But who's your complaint against, exactly? asked Solomon.
It is the wind, said the gnats, dotty speech marks, unsettled,
around nothing, and dry grass. I hear you, said Solomon, and
being swayed by your symphony, I am of a mind to take your
side. But a mediator must give ears to both sides of a story.
I, we, agree, said the twitchy, death-obsessed gnats. Summon
the East Wind, said Solomon. Jacketless as the earliest, leafiest
book, the East Wind whooshed into the outdoor court. What
of the gnats? *Gone.* Finally at one, in a wider union. The gnats'
case, summed up Solomon, is all our metaphors, so let's leave
the speech marks and agree that the sides settled their difference

far out of court, in this *Gnats v. the Wind.* My hearing. Yours.

Empty Words

The year Dad was born
a long lost trail. *Listen, yaar,*
nothing was written.

*

At home in Grasmere –
thin mountain paths have me back,
a boy in Kashmir.

*

Stratford-on-Avon.
Mum and Dad's first date; Dad's twin
kids in Pakistan.

*

Now we separate
for the first time, on our walk,
at the kissing-gate.

*

Old English 'Deor'
an exile's lament, the past's
dark, half-opened door.

*

Where migrating geese
pause to sleep – somewhere, halfway
is this pillow's crease.

*

Invader, to some –
neither here, nor there, with me –
our rhododendron.

*

'*Mate*. I was here first,'
he says, elbowing my claim
on half an armrest.

*

Fromwards . . . lost to us,
Middle English. To head back
from . . . To turn one's face.

*

The son filled *The Globe*.
The dad seamed a second skin –
stitched *V*s in the glove.

*

Yes, I know. *Empty*.
But there's just something between
the *p* and the *t*.

Stamping Grounds (Earlier)

(for their days were long before the days of photographs), my first
fancies regarding what they were like, were unreasonably derived
from their tombstones. The shape of the letters . . .
  – CHARLES DICKENS, *Great Expectations*

1

My English grandfather, whose name in my father's language
means 'land', the earliest ground I ever held was yours.
I can see it leave my fist, beneath a sleeve
of my first school blazer. The only other 'dust to dust' earth
   I've let go –
further west, twenty years on – was for Mum, who you raised
behind the counter of the Polesworth post office, on Bridge
Street; your home turf, handed down from your mother,
a sub-postmistress, who'd tap messages in Morse
and who I'd discover, years after, yards away
from that opening grave I'd stood at. And thereabouts
I'd find her parents – the Deemings – and theirs,
and theirs, and theirs, at a handful of plots, marked
and unmarked, in the grounds that ring the Abbey at Polesworth.
And later I'd hear that John Donne stayed in this same village,
in the same consecrated acre, even punning on the Earth's poles
as he rode out, mouthing lines to the East, one Good Friday
across a fading forest of Arden towards the borderlands
of the Marches – where Mum would be buried –
in days when messages went on the hoof, and by hand.

2

In these quickened times
I can't help reading POST OFFICE with the POST
first meaning 'after'; post-natal, postscript, postponed . . .
In the blank, unsorted space between other thoughts –
of Mum delaying, forever, giving you a headstone for dates
and names to cut; how, so far, I've done the same
all these years after you, and Mum, had passed on;
and how Donne's journey spanned these two graves –
something small has occurred to me. Picturing when
I first stood with Mum, as your coffin was draped with that flag
from your RAF days, I imagined a lichened slab, ivied impossibly
in later time. And there, behind the moss on *Stanley Arthur Evetts*,
the S—— A—— E—— that surely raised a comment
in passing as you signed off, in shorthand, some parcel
across the counter. To you both
it must have been as familiar as old weather in the sky
but those letters I'd never seen
are news to me – news as full as the empty tomb
to Magdalene, when the rock rolled away –
a kind of ground, or earth
I'd only picked up on today.

I

stand, unfixed, behind the name Zaffar.
And before my father left this, my land
for good, I – meaning me – asked him
why he chose my name. Mum was two
weeks from dying. Two parents would
depart that month. I hadn't spoken to
him for a decade. 'It flew into my head
in waiting room when you were born so
small and shaking. They put you in that
box. But I remembered long time back
carrying bricks in new Pakistan, maybe
thirteen years old, I left home and heard
other workers say his poetries, which I
liked. Last king of India he was. Zafar.'
First I knew of it. I'd later look into it, to
histories. The written kind. Zafar's most
famous lines, scratched onto his prison
wall, in exile, a charcoal mirror in words:
I asked for a long life. I received four days.
Two were spent in hoping. Two in waiting.
I recoiled, recalled another self-pitying: *I*
wasted time, and now doth time waste me.
After a trial for mutiny, the British lifted
this chessboard king onto a bullock cart;
on its throne he was translated. To a cell
bed in Burma. Here, his signature lament
was scored on cement with a burnt stick.
This writing on the wall winged its way
to my father's head. Historians now say
Zafar wasn't behind that waiting couplet,

his far-flown epitaph. Its sad first-person
I (its Urdu *main*) threw the voice of that
broken subject, the last king – but these
prisoned lines came later, not by his hand.
Zafar. I'd known meant 'victory'. Anyway.
Here's how that poem, by whoever, began:
Lagtaa nahii hai dil meraa ujre dayaar mei . . .
No pleasure for the heart in this derelict land . . .

Jane Austen: *Selected Letters*

1

Where shall I begin? she starts. *Which of all*
my important nothings shall I tell you first?
In her shortened sign-off, above, she'd *remain*
with Love,
         Yrs affec
            JA.

I read names into that effective absence;
Julia Ann . . . who helped shape my initial scribbles
and kept an old card with first words in my hand:
from Zaffar
        – the *ff*
             pointing backwards,

back to that consonant I couldn't then say;
stuck with my start, I was an Affer, or Faffer –
which proved true, Mum later said, of the latter.
Dawdler that I became. So here I am

taken aback by letters – their afterlife –
and how we draw together when they arrive.

2

We also talk of a Laburnam. – The Border
under the Terrace Wall is clearing away . . .

I go back and look at her second, hazier *a*
in *Laburnam*. It's you, Mum, I remember
explaining to me how a soft Indian *u*
is equally an *a*. My dad taught me to say
'Mera nam Zaffar hai'. The first vowel
in my name like the last *u* in laburnum.

As a child I'd climb that tree, spend hours lost in
its grey-green area, the high end of our garden.

Early days, at the registry in Birmingham,
Mum wrote out, in her own spelling . . . *Kunial*;
from Jat-Rajput-Kanyal – Dad's tribe or clan,
starting past those parts that talk of caste.

In *Austen*
that *A*, almost from the off   is a different sound
– more like the *o* in of   than the *u* in ground.

The Wardrobe

might be a good name for a bookshop, small but oddly ongoing,
the kind you'd happen upon, and enter, perhaps alone, perhaps
not, in a long grown-up coat. And as you place your cold hand
in its gloveless pocket, and feel the tweed edges of empty space
you might be reminded – as I am – of a sleeved scene in a book;
a scene I knew firstly from a VHS film I'd replay, by the fire, rapt
as a kid, watching Lucy's cartoon fingers push through long fur
coats – further, touching branches. Snow. I don't know about you
but I never forgot this feeling I've never had – like that episode
of sleeplessness in a book I did read later, spellbound, where a fir
branch, tapping a gusty window, was never fir, but skin and bone;
Cathy's icy ghost hand: *I'm come home.* Gripped, gripping, through

the broken glass. On top of the MDF wardrobe near the landing
fittingly high from the ground, was our family's Quran, wrapped
in cloth. Gilt-edged, wide enough to house three scripts. Around
the time I'd be glued to films like *The Lion, the Witch . . .* I'd place
a chair beneath, take down the shrouded weight, undo the black
sleeve, open a page and read a corridor of the English that slept
in the margins. I wasn't sure why I did this, or what I'd fear
I might miss, or if I was sitting the right way, or how to feel true
to the words. I'd lift them back, rewrapped, onto the wardrobe.
Distantly, I've long looked up to books. The distance they cover.
Picture me, delayed, walking through a bookshop – say this one
– forgetting what I first came in for, or if I ever really knew

The Lyric Eye

Methinks I see these things with parted eye
– WILLIAM SHAKESPEARE, *A Midsummer Night's Dream*

I've stood at your portrait at different times.
Scanned my own face, on and off, in the glass.
A cloud, eclipsed. Vaguely before, or behind
you. Half cast, at a loss.

               Even the gloss
back then, at school, left me looking this blank.
In the dark. Not on the same page as you.

But when I stand, here, almost in a blink
I can place my eyes – glazed over your stare;
let you lend me your ear, your famous cheek;
let the flare of your nostril stretch thin air;
even try on your earring, from five feet,
four centuries apart. I swear   by this lapse
the light on your mouth seems cast

                          half on mine
when I borrow the line between your lips.

Self Portrait as Bottom

O I am translated.
The speech of numbers.
Here's me in them
and them in me. I spat
into the bottom of a test tube,
gob upon gob, and posted it
to a lab across the Irish Sea.
But before I dropped
it all in their SAE
I stared at that shiny
alembic's elongated U
and saw an elongated
face of me, staring past
my drool, trying to summon
– or glue, the way spit
does a stamp – the unconnected
unspeaking dead. Me. Or so
the science and the blurb says.
Let's get down to numbers.
What could be more prosaic?
I am split. *50% Europe.*
50% Asia. Figures that speak
to me and feel
like a thousand-year stare.
But the numbers, from *thousands*
of years ago didn't end there.
18% of me is from the narrow
island they call *Great Britain*
and then, just less, *17% Ireland*;
8% Europe West; *3% Scandinavia*;

3% Finland/Northwest Russia.
And *1% Italy/Greece*, labyrinthine
lands of the minotaur, and the Fates
as weavers, and the lost thread.
And from my dad?
48% Asia South. Which as good
as says that my father's
folk were converts in the near
past, perhaps lower caste, perhaps
believers in the many, in sky gods
cast in Sanskrit, or heavy Buddha,
or puckish forest figures,
winged gandharvas.
And the last *2%* of my father's
half is from what they call
Asia West, or *Caucasus*,
which is anywhere above
the Himalayas to the Black Sea,
and almost meets
Mum's small Italian/Greek,
but not quite.
And this bit, the almost meeting,
I've felt at some level,
a low level, mutteringly,
a kind of abysmal underneathness
or usness, under the heights
of language, which, ridiculously
I looked to see in that U-
shaped test tube, through
saliva's bubbled glass,
and to see it face to face
and not only in part,
or passing, or past.

And Farther Again

The motif, 'Three Hares', each chasing the scut
of his dead-spit in front, is tricky in terms
of provenance;

catchable as Scotch mist, or haar out to sea,
it's been traced to the Silk Road
and farther again,

tracked to the heels of the Sui Dynasty,
as a hieroglyph, as it happens,
of the verb

'to be'. It's on Mongol metalwork and a coin
from Iran that just missed Rumi's
hand, dated 1281.

It's a Christian sign too, an echo of eternity
or the trinity; again, hard to pin
down, or put an *x*

where this began. Whether bossed at crossed vaults
in gothic churches, or inlaid in floors,
see how the three

rotating hares share ears in common; heads linked
in the round, like the dots that eye
the teardrops in the Yin

and Yang. And now our words are of China,
I put a 'Three Hares' tile into your hand –
a gift that finds

a void – like the gaps within the mould. But its old
circular theme, set inside a square,
gets me thinking of Escher,

how the far ground becomes the fore, a fugue
that little Zaphyr could trace
around and draw.

And as you're telling me that a nail won't get far
in the stone bricks above your door,
it brings up the three-

chaired counselling the two of us undertook;
how each hour was a strange loop –
where split hairs went

back and forth, over a hook, a theme to our patterns,
the gaps in the listening, repeated
to no end. So

it's hard now to hear it, and from the mother of my son;
you put the tile down, we can't get back,
you've moved. On.

The Still

My wealth let sons and brethren part.
Some things they cannot share:
my work well done, my noble heart,
these are mine own to wear.
　　　 – JABIR (attrib.), the 'first practical alchemist'

You'll know, Son, of the Jabberwock
and may even feel fear,
but what of Ibn Hayyan
whose pen-name was Jabir?

He scrawled in ciphers, an algebra,
a hush-hush way of talking
that kept cloaked his experiments
in (whisper it) *takwin* –

the haram quest to fashion life –
alchemical recipes
to make scorpions, snakes and humans
which helped Mary conceive

of *Frankenstein*, shadowed in *Faust*.
Quietly his work still lasts,
from 'the ashes' of our *alkalis*
to our distilling flasks,

his own retort and *alembic* –
or *al anbiq*, 'the still' –
in which I see English *amber*;
like a wrong speech bubble . . .

But Jabir trapped the essence of time
and proved alcohol's need
in this golden-age caliphate
of Haroun al-Rashid –

the base wine of poets distilled
for his pure, helpful djinn;
scents seal their notes with this spirit
and inks seal their nights in . . .

*

Darkly, there's Jabir – up late, in his lab
scrying retorts of mist,
mulling on how time might preserve him –
muttering *gibberish*.

Just a Minute

The whereabouts of things has gone, but I
can see the radio on the right, as you
rummage in a drawer. Same side as the sink. I
can't reach up to the stiff tap, as Birmingham
water drums against that hollow tin base. I am
splashed by what you say rushed down Welsh hills
to this cupboarded corridor, the tightest room –
All is at hand, you'd add – in our Tardis metre

      here, from our narrow, clapped-out kitchen
      above trapped voices, the running
      tap, the hammering accents of water.

Still reaching, I turn as you explain the radio's cue:
To speak, without hesitation, deviation,
or repetition.   One subject. This span.   Undoable
I think. Like swimming a length. Small, stammering –

      the rules of the game rule out all my talk – even
      inside. A pause traps every impossible time.
      A drawer that holds a drawer that holds a

      Wait. Any second she'll be there. Listen.   You

turn off the tap to cheers as the whistle blows.
Our laughter outlasts the long wave's applause.

Q

Somewhere (thank you, Father) over the hills,
through some half-door in my mind, despite my having
no call to speak it, and hearing of it so long ago,
I know the Urdu *ishq* is love.
And further, how it's the highest (a divine fervour,
a bolt cued from the round heavens – almost angelic)
among a whole host of forms, or feathers, of love
like that story of subtle Inuit measures of snow

and now I've *utterly gone and put my foot in it*
and other shoppers are turning round, as we inch
up to the queue's end, still far from those tills
and she's prodding me to explain my mute, short-falling
answer – giving a nod, when she asked me *If* . . . and *Whether* . . .
– she swears, that at the end of my assent she heard me whisper
-ish

Tall Kahani

*Straight answers were beyond the powers of Rashid Khalifa,
who would never take a short cut if there was a longer, twistier
road available.*
    – SALMAN RUSHDIE, *Haroun and the Sea of Stories*

As bucket is to balti
so batty are the mad Bauls.
As quickly is to jaldi
a Qawwaal is a Sufi who calls.

As tale is to kahani
and lambi far too tall
so safar is our far journey
as sab is to everything. That's all.

But, Dad, *sab* is our word for partly or under.
And to *safar* is to be under strife.
And if *kaha* means 'where', and *nahii* means 'no',
then is *kahani* – your 'story' – from nowhere?

No, Son.
Only if your story is broken.
As zindagi is too.

Dad – go on – don't break off.
What's *zindagi*? Or what's it like?
What's the story there?

That, my son, is just life.

Luck

Unused, as yet,
and left. Locked.
All the weight of a hand
if a hand wasn't held.

And brand new keys.
There are three in the loop;
two spares, if one were
for keeps.

But nothing is. Not even this
heavy-hearted padlock –
the shackled U as bright as changed luck –
chucked, maybe dropped

among leaves and crisp packets in the road;
today's silver-lined present
fished up from the kerb,
a catch in its throat.

Liquidity

In a dictionary I look the other way, down its page
to one of the five entries of 'LIST,
v. the tilt of a ship' – 'a variant of earlier *lust*.'
Two letters hold the balance. I dwell on unsteady edges –
of the economy, and of Europe, and Greece
and evasively changing the subject, via Syracuse, or Sicily,
an old treatise . . .

Across the water –
Bahr-i-Sefid, *the Sea of White*
to some, and to others *Our Sea*, Mare Nostrum –

in Constantinople, on 10th-century goatskin, a parchment
of prayers was found at the turn of the last
century. The recovered prayers above turned out to be the least

valuable thing, for under the clearer ink
lay the difficult-to-see words of Archimedes'
On Floating Bodies. And each letter
in their first coinage –
not the Latin of the coming empire
but the governing language of Greater Greece.

Even in translation, these theorems
that settled the subject of displacement
had been out of sight
and to our long, unwritten future
almost entirely lost.

Rainglobe

The warl' like an eemis stane
Wags i' the lift
— HUGH MACDIARMID

in this tilted
storm-knocked world –

this drop of Earth
that holds the lift –

how can we secure
the cobblestones to the coastal fog

or believe   that above the whirl
of cloud and flood

we might see – through whorls
on this stony sky –

the smudged wobble-handed
fingerprints of love

warl' – world;   *eemis stane* – unsteady stone;   *lift* – sky

Stamping Grounds (Later)

Could I behold those hands which span the poles . . .
– JOHN DONNE, 'Good Friday, 1613, Riding Westward'

My English grandfather. Stanley. Stan.
The first ground I ever held was yours.
I can see the earth leave my fist, beneath a sleeve
of my first school blazer. Further west, twenty years
after, the only other handful of earth I've let go
was for Mum, who you raised behind the counter

of the Polesworth post office on Bridge Street
in that village you'd be buried in. The same village
John Donne saddled up in, one Good Friday,
riding westwards towards the Welsh Marches –
where Mum would be buried – in days
when messages went on the hoof, and by hand.

In these unsaddled, unsolid, quickened times
I read the words POST OFFICE with the POST
first meaning 'after'; post-millennial, post-dated . . .
In the blank, unsorted space between other thoughts
something has occurred to me   I picture you
signing your name on what passes across a small changed

counter – Stanley Arthur Evetts – and there it is, writ large
in your imagined hand   SAE   To you and Mum
it must have been as familiar as old weather in the sky
but those first letters are new ground to me. As I stand
on a planet you've both passed from, it's like a present
in the post – a coin of earth – held up to this day.

Empty Words

Meaning 'homeland' – *mulk*
(in Kashmir) – exactly how
my son demands milk.

*

Full-rhyme with *Jhelum*,
the river nearest his home –
my father's 'realm'.

*

Mouthing the word *mouse*
what escapes me is the 'thief'
in the Sanskrit *mus*.

*

You can't put a leaf
between *written* and *oral*;
that first 'A', or 'alif'.

*

Letters. West to east
Mum's hand would write; Dad's script goes
east to west. Received.

*

A for apple. Y
for Yggdrasil, Odin's ash
which echoes with twig.

*

'. . . slow / Horse. The color
of trust.' Wait. She wrote *rust*. From
nowhere, a letter.

*

Something's missing here –
a sixth sense, between forests
and hues . . . *Sylva?*

*

Birch – an alpha *b*
back when branch-like runes mothered
the words from the trees.

*

Boc. Boc, says my son.
A bark up the right tree . . . 'Book'/
'beech' were once bound. One.

*

The night Max wore his
wolf suit . . . I begin again
in my oldest voice.

The Long Causeway

We are driving higher and higher,
twisted steepness holding my hand to first gear;
some homesick, star-hung satellite making me climb
Smithy Lane, skyward, to Blackshaw Head, in a hired red Aygo.

Continue straight ahead. Which is not easy down here,
up and around the next bend. On black ice. *Boom boom boom*
Even brighter than the moon moon moon. Turning down the radio
so I can hear the satnav, and myself think . . . *'Cause baby*

you're a firework – all this time, catching sight of a stick
swoosh in and out the windscreen mirror – I ask my boy,
whose car-seat faces back, if he's playing a game. *I'm making*
things happen, Daddy. Rounding the corner, the green dark

edge is taken off the horizon as we go over the tops.
On the turn is a white page, more defined than the lost sheep
and hill clouds. *I'm Jack Frost*, he says. And behind
that cold stick he'd picked up in the woods – like a new word

in the mirror, I see the brushstroke of a black road, tapered
to a point backwards – then before it, I see flashed
what was a 'sword'; that twig he'd seen to the hilt as gold
and now is differently sharp – a wand, delicate and moon-tipped:

conducting the snow's dance, beyond the stick's flourished
end, on a half-hidden Long Causeway.
I'm slowing now, to a stop.
                                    Snow-wand, sword, branch; whatever
it is – the wave of it, or the first particle at its point –

paints all that is behind us   with all that lay ahead.

Six

Forget that old joke about   timing, which I won't rudely
repeat. I learnt that timing had a world to do with weight
transference between the feet, planting my front pole
down, and as the ball is middled, the burden on the back
foot amasses through the axis of tensed, stick-thin arms
to the sweet spot in the rootless willow. A kind of sacrifice

from one side to the other. The ball now hit, and staying
hit – airborne, insanely towards a sky the locked-in
Scottish grandmother I'd never meet might have called
the lift. Over the fence, from that first garden
to another address, all that wound-up string beneath
the skin. Gone. *Mum's gone*, says Roseta, the girl at 60,

next to our 58, one morning while fetching the washing
from a line spiralling a shared stake. *Gone where?*
asks mine. *Where's your mother?   She's dead? Dear God,
o Love*, Mum says above the crossed lines. At her tears
I'm still cottoning on. Roseta, Zeta, who posted
my first Valentine, signed with a question mark I'd not

get. Whose mum was *the only one* who could get me
to sleep. To the country of that eternal beginningness.
She'd come round in the small hours, Mum would say,
*hearing your cries, Dad working nights, and she'd go
like this, jigging you in her arms, and you'd be off, gone.*
She'd come from Barbados, her husband from Jamaica,

a one-time boxer; *different islands, different tempers*,
she'd tell Mum. Fighting leaked in and past walls.
Silences too. Belted up. Once, innocent, naked,
I placed my penis through that fence, peed – till he waved
a pitchfork; fathers fist-fought. Once, Zeta's dad shook
a crowbar. Mine raised Mum's school hockey stick.

Dad's middle finger smashed. Feeling gone. Forever.
He made me press a needle to test the dead, knuckled
centre. The nerves.   Gone. The word's weight returns
me to that fenced world, at this turning point, when
my bat arcs up, held high, the sun weightless in the glass
of next door's greenhouse. A perfect still point, until it's all

gone sharp. Loud as the pitch of a pole star. And the sky falls
in.

A Drink at the Door

That's what I'm reading here. I mean the Dickens.
That and some downloaded contemporary
I keep switching from, on my lighted Kindle.
But it's not the light that came with this reader
and candles the cold, framed screen; it's the trick
of the light in this pub that detains me.
And not in this place alone. What is it
this yellowed, well-thumbed light has borrowed from?
By a less lonely table, a dog's ear
twitches. Somehow the glow pooled round my pew
hosts its own table talk. As mahogany
is a wood of a certain age, so too
this light is dated, refracted by it
and the dark matter that's caked in the grain.
And it's refracted, beyond that, by smoke
at the back of this malt, death and life mixed,
as familiar as a browned penny,
particular as fog. And it picks up
a dim street in Dickens, a door that gives
to this light, refracted here by the din
and the sharp bark of that dog. The Bear.
That was it. Dad's early haunt. Those big doors
that looked locked. And there, ensconced, hours later,
the same filament in frosted, smoked glass.

*

Like a burr stuck in the folds of my scarf,
this light has trailed me longer than I knew.
Out there, the darkness also has a hand
in these refractions. That and the bitter
cold I'm in from. If I keep losing you,
please bear with the thought of light. Like this shot
of malt bears its long, peat finish, sea-noted, late . . .
There's a low fire breathing, and an argument
somewhere. And I've come to an inn. In Orkney.
1824. In his Irish burr,
I hear the landlord attempt to intervene.
Four generations later, his descendent
pokes at the grate of his pub in Aberdeen.
And his wayward daughter asks for a light
in a West Midlands asylum, home for life.
And her daughter, between trains, wanders out
to Needless Alley, looks in at The Windsor,
catching the eye of my eventual father.
Shortly they'll see, in this same light, they share
the one brand of cigarette.
                                    The refractions
will go on, past my stay; I'm only here
for one. A drink at the door. A last drop
trails down the glass. I'll pack my Kindle away.
Exit this light that has taken me in.

Us

If you ask me, *us* takes in *undulations* –
each wave in the sea, all insides compressed –
as if, from one coast, you could reach out to

the next; and maybe it's a Midlands thing
but when I was young, *us* equally meant *me*,
says the one, 'Oi, you, tell us where yer from';

and the way supporters share the one fate –
I, being one, am *Liverpool* no less –
cresting the Mexican wave of *we* or *us*,

a shore-like state, two places at once, God
knows what's in it; and, at opposite ends
my heart's sunk at separations of *us*.

When it comes to us, colour me unsure.
Something in me, or it, has failed the course.
I'd love to think I could stretch to it – us –

but the waves therein are too wide for words.
I hope you get, here, where I'm coming from.
I hope you're with me on this – between love

and loss – where I'd give myself away, stranded
as if the universe is a matter of one stress.
Us. I hope, from here on, I can say it

and though far-fetched, it won't be too far wrong.

Ys

I've been a long time that I'm waiting
– NICK DRAKE, 'Northern Sky'

It was Monday, bank holiday, near the end
of May, rough middle of the day, year, and
of the country if the country is England.
Oak Apple, or Oak and Nettle Day, axis of my year
thinly plotted as my tree – the far end of our
thinning garden, in a border shaped to waver
like a child's drawing of sea – its clockhanded Y
where the trunk parted ways, a first rung that even
just turned seven I step onto, into the above,
this wobbly earth above earth. Wordlessly
I knew then, I'd later be gone, like possibly
my tree has, from that border, and my attention
divided thinly as the light, or is that time, through
the green-grey space I was sitting in as I
reached up   for a branch, or is it balance, or
vantage? on this tentative level.   A story

. . .

I can see myself in or on, just, nearly.
Almost. Its yearly trick. The sticking place.
I can reconfigure it in my head, that first
page, and the first word, that M and y
in the first novel I read. Nineteen.
Begun just before we left the house –
with the tree that was always there – finished
elsewhere. Mum left Dad in the summer
between school's end and the future. No literature.
Story books weren't for me till this late.
Or soon. But begin it did, literature and me.
My name is Karim Amir, and I am an Englishman born and bred,
almost. In my book the line break was there.
It – or English lit. – had me at almost.

. . .

Hwær cwom mearg? Hwær cwom mago?
Where is the horse gone? Where the young man?
Uuere beþ þey biforen vs weren?
Where are those who were before us?
Hwær becomes *Uuere* becomes my *where*.
Where's gone Daddy? To the country called Back Home.
When is he back here? 'Autumn.' *Is that tomorrow?*
'No, Son.' *So today?* 'No, Son.' Wise now, Mum pointed
through the nicotine-brown window. 'When all the leaves
fall from your tree.' The laburnum had bloomed
its yellow envelope in my birthday week. *When
will a present come?* had become *when's the lello flowers?*
The tree held court in that laburnum time
before letters stuck, like Dad, his story of when
he came here and stared up at shop signs
on Stratford Road – learning the shapes and the wares.

. . .

Nothing else would do. Autumn. October. Another season. Months.
Moons. Later that summer I saw through the living room window a
strange breeze shaking your birthday *tree, nothing else moving – only*
what we called your tree, down the end of the lawn – like something
mythical. When you went I felt you'd gone to a place like that, a shap-
ing place. *What I hadn't seen was a small boy who understood even less*
than I thought, time on his little hands, I can feel the powdery bark
now, pushing in the border *between summer and autumn, looking up*

to see leaves
in their bowl
of full branches
hold time – not fall
as if stuck on purpose
. . . Disturbing the dust on
the bark was making you sneeze –
trust you to be allergic to your tree. Heaven
knows why you'd always want to step into it later on.

But before you can remember, I watched you shake your tree with all
your weight. You came in with eyes streaming and swollen, the intervals
between breaths tight, *wheezing, asking why the tree wouldn't let Daddy*
come back. A fortnight later or was it more? the letter I posted would have
arrived, a first letter to your dad, on pale blue airmail paper, a folding

envelope of a letter, and your dad says that when he read the cramped words, posted from a red pillar box I'd guess, on the same road where he learned to read English, *about how you pushed at what you didn't understand* – with all my weight, and more besides – *as if shaking all the green out of your tree would fetch your dad out of a blue sky, and how you pushed and stared up*

up into the stubborn
shadows and shapes between
the branches, *it made him cry, into*
the black ink he was reading – and it's your
telling of this I see and in each telling I'd imagine
the story, unfolding again, my memory shading into yours,

into the tree with the low fork, into times I sat in it, hid in its crooked space, absent-mindedly rubbing my eyes in the tree's dust – *till it all blurred*, every clear thing under later, unvisited weather, blotting into an English cloud. A grey smudge on a faint blue leaf. The last shape I see, in this fabled cloud of English, is the wide-armed first letter of

Yours
remaining
under a vanishing
story, past all that yields
in time and all that won't, ever –
unpushable as a tree's clockwork – its *ours*
and whatever's up, above it, is unreadable. The sky,
at this illegible legendary stage, always becomes a thin blue-

grey page, held in my father's hands. One sky like tracing paper, held above another. Held above a laburnum.